THE WEDGE BOOK

THE WEDGE BOOK

by
DOUG FORD

**PREFACE BY
JULIUS BOROS**

Published by  CORNERSTONE, LIBRARY, INC.
NEW YORK

Reprinted 1966

Illustrations by James McQueen

CORNERSTONE LIBRARY PUBLICATIONS
Are Distributed by
Affiliated Publishers
A Division of Pocket Books, Inc.
630 Fifth Avenue, New York, N. Y. 10020

Manufactured in the United States of America
under the supervision of
Rolls Offset Printing Co., Inc., N. Y.

PREFACE

BY JULIUS BOROS

Doug Ford and I have a lot in common. We were both born in Connecticut a little over 40 years ago, and we both began our professional golf careers in 1949 after lengthy stints as amateurs.

We worked our way up on the pro circuit amid some pretty fine company—Jackie Burke, Ted Kroll, Tommy Bolt and Jerry Barber, to name a few, arrived about the same time. Doug Ford and I both feel that the current crop of young golfers, including Arnold Palmer, Gary Player, Jack Nicklaus and Tony Lema, is the best to come up since that group of a decade ago.

But despite the tough, new competition, I predict Doug Ford will have at least five or ten more successful years on the tour if he wants them. He has great desire and is a keen competitor. Beyond that, he is a great wedge player. When you can play wedge shots like Doug Ford does, you are going to stay in contention on the tournament circuit.

Few pros, if any, can match Doug's record of consistently fine performances during the last dozen years. He is durable, a talented scorer, and at the week's end can always be found at the pay window. Besides that, he is a fine gentleman, a family man and a credit to professional golf.

What Doug Ford has to say about hitting wedge shots has to be accepted as "bible." No golfer can go wrong by following his advice. Look at what he has done with the wedge. He is good with every club in the bag but, above all, his skill with the wedge has helped him carve a great golf career.

Doug is equally effective with a pitching wedge or a sand wedge.

I remember the 1962 Bing Crosby tournament when Doug tied for first with Joe Campbell. On the first hole of the sudden death playoff, Doug hit his approach shot into a trap and it looked like he was finished. But he pulled out the sand wedge and exploded to within six feet of the hole. Then, as Campbell was three-putting from the distant front edge of the green, Doug rapped in his putt to win first prize money.

Few players can get down in two the way Doug Ford can. In this book he tells you how he does it. It can help you do the same.

Fort Lauderdale, Fla.
September, 1963.
Julius Boros

INTRODUCTION

MEET DOUG FORD

Doug Ford's confidence and ability with the pitching wedge was displayed in the final round of the New York Metropolitan Open one year.

On the 16th hole, standing five under par, he hooked his drive into the rough. When he got to the ball, Doug found himself waiting for a slow-moving threesome that was still lining up putts on the green. Doug could easily have reached the green with a No. 5 iron, but he likes to play fast. Rather than wait until the men ahead had putted out, he pulled out his wedge and intentionally played 70 yards short of the green—apparently certain he could get down in two from there. And he did it—with a great wedge approach that almost hit the pin, and an easy tap-in putt for his par.

Doug Ford has a golf gift that appears only occasionally in several generations—incredible accuracy from just off the green. Not since Johnny Revolta, 25 years ago, has there been a player who can "get down in two" as often from within 100 yards of the hole.

7

Doug was born 41 years ago in New Haven, Conn., and grew up in New York City where his father was a driving range pro. Doug was introduced to golf at the age of six and found his father's range a convenient place to practice in his early years.

He was an outstanding third-baseman in semi-pro baseball and was offered a scholarship to Manhattan College. But when he won the New York Junior golf title, he decided that golf was his sport.

Later, after winning the Westchester County and New York Amateur championships, he toured the pro circuit for two years as an amateur trying to decide whether his game was strong enough to meet the competition. It held up, and then some. He turned pro in 1949, at the age of 27, and has been among the top ten money winners ten times since 1951. No other pro can match this record and only three active tournament players—Sam Snead, Cary Middlecoff and Arnold Palmer—have won more tournaments than Ford.

Doug's biggest victories were in the 1955 PGA Championship and in the 1957 Masters. He is only one of a handful of golfers who have captured both of these major titles. More recently, Doug has won the 1959 and 1963 Canadian Open, the 1960 and 1961 "500" Festival Open, the 1962 Bing Crosby National and the 1962 Eastern Open. In 1955, he was named professional "Player of the Year" and was a member of the U.S. Ryder Cup teams in 1955, 1957, 1959 and 1961. He is considered one of the most durable professionals on the tour.

Twice he has been the tour's No. 2 money winner, earning $26,815 in 1953 and $45,378 in 1957.

Gifted with a sense of humor and a knack for making

his words do a lot of work, Doug said after winning the Pensacola Open one year, "This is a great victory for scramblers. There aren't many of us scrapers left."

Former U. S. champion Ed Furgol once said: "There are about 25 golfers on the tour who can play as well as Doug, but Doug has the interest, enthusiasm and spirit they lack. He loves everything about the game of golf."

In the 1957 Pensacola tournament, Doug teed off in the third round and shot an astounding 45 on the first nine holes. Everyone was stunned.

"Are you sick, Doug?" they asked.

"Heck no," he replied. "I'm all right. It's just that I stubbed my toe on the television set last night."

What happened after that 45 partly explains Ford's success. He played the back nine in 35 and then fired a 68 in the final round to finish in the money.

That's typical of Doug Ford—finishing in the money. In this book he tells you how to use the club that is chiefly responsible.

Gerard J. Pfarr, Associate Editor
Golf Digest

CONTENTS

Preface by Julius Boros
Introduction—Meet Doug Ford

CHAPTER	PAGE
1 Meet the Wedge—A Friend	17
2 Grip, Stance and Swing	27
3 The Pitch Shot	33
4 High and Low—Cut and Punch	37
5 Trouble? Wedge!	43
6 More Trouble Shots	51
7 The Right Sand Wedge for You	61
8 The Basic Sand Shot	129
9 Sand, Sand Everywhere	135
10 Trouble Shots from Sand	141
11 Be a Tiger!	149
12 Chatting About Golf	155

ILLUSTRATIONS

	PAGE
Comparing the 9-iron, the pitching and the sand wedge	20
"Feeling" the wedge shot for distance and roll	24
The proper stance	28
The proper grip	28
Addressing a short pitch shot	30
The Pitch Shot: address and backswing	34
The Pitch Shot: impact and follow through	35
The Punch Shot	38
The Cut Shot	40
The wedge in heavy rough	46
Comparing the normal pitch shot to the shot from heavy rough	47
Hitting the wedge from tall grass	53
Hitting a plugged ball	56
Putting the "ride" and flanged sole of the sand wedge to work for you	58
Comparing the "ride" of the sand wedge to that of the pitching wedge	62
Opening up the face of the sand wedge	131
Hitting out of different types of sand	137
Normal, uphill and downhill lies	143
Ball below feet and ball above feet	144
Wet sand	145
Buried Lie	145
Plugged lie	146
Buried lie	146
Putting and chipping	147

PHOTOGRAPHS

	PAGE
Blasting from a sand trap with accuracy	16
Doug Ford at the Los Angeles Open	26
A 75-yard pitch shot drops in	32
The 1957 Ryder Cup Team	36
Out of the trap to win the 1962 Crosby Invitational	42
A big splash at the 1957 Masters	50
The 1955 PGA Champion in action	60
Animated Instruction Section	65-127
Getting out of sand at the Insurance City Open	134
Practicing with the sand wedge	140
The competitive determination of Doug Ford	150
The match play victor of the 1955 PGA Championship	154
The "green jacket" ceremony at the 1958 Masters	157

THE WEDGE BOOK

Doug Ford, one of golf's greatest wedge players and money winners, blasts from a trap and the ball pops onto the green and near the pin.

Chapter One

Meet the Wedge — A Friend

Of all the iron clubs, the pitching wedge is probably the most often used. This is particularly true of better players who have confidence in the club and can play more difficult and different shots with it than a novice can.

The wedge can be used with accuracy from its maximum distance of about 100 yards all the way down to within a yard or two of the green under certain circumstances.

It can be used for many types of chip shots—lofted chips, running chips and all kinds in between.

The pitching wedge also can be used to hit from a sand trap but a sand wedge usually is preferable. There is actually no telling how many shots can be executed with the pitching wedge if the golfer has control of the club and knows what he is doing.

This book will cover most of the normal shots possible with both wedges, plus many of the more uncommon situations where these shots become an invaluable addition to your golfing repertoire. It will also discuss when not to use the wedge, and some of the common errors that novices make with the club.

THE "CONFIDENCE" CLUB

The wedge is considered one of the most important clubs because it is used mostly in the scoring zone—from 75 or 100 yards on into the green—where a person has the most opportunity to "save" shots. A good shot with the wedge can preserve a par or bag a birdie. A bad wedge stroke can mean a bogey, or worse.

The pitching wedge is frequently used by the average player because he misses more greens in regulation figures with the other clubs than does the professional. He lands just off the green at least as often as he lands on it.

Before 1932, the niblick actually performed the services the wedge does now. But it was never as effective, especially in sand traps. During the winter of 1932, Gene Sarazen fashioned a club with a heavily flanged sole. With this club he was able to "blast" out of a sand trap within ten feet of the pin. This newly developed sand iron was the forerunner of the present-day wedge.

I think the wedge is the greatest asset to scoring in golf today. It is the major weapon professionals use to reduce scoring and many have perfected it to a science. The wedge, since its invention, has been *the* club in the bag. It's the club that has been the chief factor in low scoring throughout the years.

Because of its tremendous importance, all golfers should learn to use the wedge as expertly as possible. They shouldn't let the club frighten them. They should practice the wedge shot until it becomes commonplace and good shots become second nature. That's the way it is with the pros. They have hit so many great wedge shots they can't even remember most of them.

The one I remember best happened back in about 1946 when I was playing a friendly amateur match at the Miami Country Club. The match had become quite heated and finally hinged on a 70-yard pitch to the 18th green. It was really an impossible kind of shot—to an elevated green with the pin up close to the front edge. My job was to throw it up there high and stop it on the front edge. I made the shot and it stopped about eight inches from the hole for the birdie that won the match.

That was the shot that started me thinking seriously about going on the tour. I had been practicing such shots for years and this time I pulled it off under extreme pressure. I have always felt that it made me become a professional golfer.

Every player on the tournament circuit today is great with the wedge. The only difference is that some can play only straightaway wedges while others can also "finesse" under extreme conditions. The best players can manuever the ball and get it up close for one putt even when the shot requires some trickery or an exceptional touch.

VITAL STATISTICS

Let's take a look at the club itself and see what makes it different from the other clubs in your bag. First, there is normally about three or four degrees more loft in the pitching wedge than in the 9-iron. The sand wedge, on the other hand, has three or four more degrees of loft than the pitching wedge. The wedges are also about half an inch shorter in shaft length than the nine iron and are a good bit heavier. Usually there is ¼ ounce difference in weight between consecutive irons. That is, an 8-iron is approximately ¼ ounce heavier than the 7-iron and the 9-iron is ¼ ounce

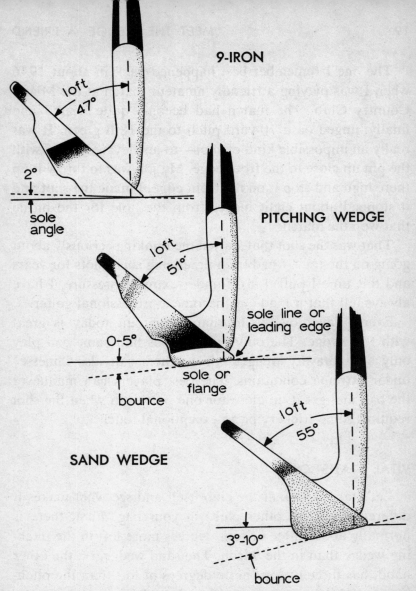

9-IRON

loft 47°

2°

sole angle

PITCHING WEDGE

loft 51°

sole line or leading edge

0-5°

sole or flange

bounce

SAND WEDGE

loft 55°

3°-10°

bounce

Unlike the 9-iron, the pitching and sand wedges have an angle of bounce that gives them their riding qualities through turf and sand. They won't dig in as much as a 9-iron.

heavier than the 8-iron. But the wedges are normally a full ounce heavier than the 9-iron, and the sand wedge is usually, but not always, a bit heavier than the pitching wedge.

What really makes the difference though is the sole and sole line of the wedges. They have what is called a "flanged" sole. This flange, or sole, actually extends below the horizontal in these clubs and results in what we call an amount or degree of "bounce."

A 9-iron (or any other iron) will have the back edge of the sole level with or even higher than the front when the club is set down in a normal address position. In the wedges, the back end of the sole is actually lower than the front or leading edge.

"Bounce" gives wedges their "riding" qualities—through the turf in the case of the pitching wedge and through the sand in the case of the sand wedge. In other words, these clubs will not dig in as deeply as a 9-iron. Thus, wedges give a more consistent performance. The leading edge of the sand wedge is even more rounded than that of the pitching wedge. This gives the player an extra measure of safety that the clubhead will not cut too deeply into the sand and thus lose too much clubhead speed.

DETERMINING YOUR MAXIMUM DISTANCE

One of the first things a golfer should do when mastering a wedge is to learn the maximum distance at which he can use it accurately. My own personal limit is about 100 yards. The only time I will ever try to use the pitching wedge for greater distance than that is when I have a following wind and must hit over a bunker to a hard green. I might try to ride the wind with a high shot, but even then it's a gamble. It's more of a "hope" shot than a tried and true shot.

Naturally some golfers hit wedges farther than do others. I doubt that the average golfer should attempt to use it for more than 80 or 90 yards. But go out on a practice range, or on the course, determine your maximum distance and learn to judge it under varying conditions. I find that many golfers with whom I play in pro-amateur events are consistently short of the target with full wedge shots, merely because they think they can hit them farther than they actually can.

Somebody asked me recently, "Doug, what is a good wedge shot? How close to the hole should I be stopping them before I'm satisfied?"

Well, this varies with amateurs, depending on their ability and how far they have progressed with the game. Some will be doing well to hit a 50-yard wedge shot on the green. Others—those who can break 90—should be knocking a 50-yard shot within 20 or 25 feet of the hole so they can almost always get down in two putts at the most. Now and then they'll get within 10 feet and have a good crack at a birdie.

The pros, I think, when hitting from about 50 yards out, should get the ball within 10 or 12 feet. And we should be almost as consistent from 75 yards as we are from 50. A real good wedge player will get inside 10 or 12 feet every time—often within 5 feet on greens that are soft enough to hold shots that land by the hole.

What is the farthest *you* should hit a wedge shot?

Here's how you can determine that for yourself. Take the wedge out and hit it to its full capacity—maybe that's 90 or 100 yards, as hard as you can hit. Then work back in towards the green until you get to an area where you have good control with the club. This is usually a half or three-quarter shot, maybe 50 or 75 yards. That should be your maximum distance. When you're stretching a shot past its maximum, you're sacrificing accuracy.

You'll find amateurs and pros who use the wedge for shots of 90 or 100 yards, or more. But that's risky for the average player. At these distances he has to swing so hard with the wedge that he's sacrificing control.

Here is another word of advice: Start with a wedge that isn't quite as heavy as normal. In this way, you can get a better feel of the club and how the ball reacts on these short shots without being burdened by the extra weight of this club.

Since the wedge is used so much for recovery shots and around the green, where you are likely to have many different types of lies, it is a club that requires a lot of practice. You have to learn what the club will do and what shots you have the ability to play. A wedge shot should never be a guess shot. It should be a shot you have practiced and played before.

PLOTTING SHORTER SHOTS AND ROLL

The best way to practice short shots with the pitching wedge is to stand behind a bunker about 10 or 20 yards from the edge of the green. Then discover through trial and error just how much power it takes to get the ball to the green. Then move farther out until you reach your maximum distance for accurate shots.

To determine how far a ball will roll, you should practice

landing the ball on a specific spot. A shag bag makes an excellent "pin" because it can be placed at different positions on the green. You can practice hitting short of this target from various distances and then note how far the ball rolls in each case.

I have a rule of thumb that I use on short wedge shots to the green. I figure to fly the ball about two-thirds of the way and let it run the rest of the way to the hole. Of course, on longer and higher wedge shots, which carry some backspin, the ball won't roll as far.

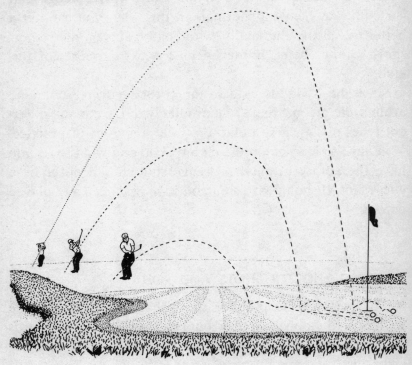

Practicing pitching to a green from various distances will give you a "feel" as to how hard these shots should be hit and how far they will roll.

With practice you'll learn how much roll you can expect on a 20-yard wedge shot, a 40-yard shot, a 60-yard shot and so on—to a green of normal texture. After that, you can pick the spot on the green where you want the ball to land and then aim for it with predictable results.

Using the pitching wedge to make his recovery shot in Los Angeles Open, Doug Ford gets the ball close enough to the hole for a one-putt. A potential bogey became a par.

Chapter Two

Grip, Stance
And Swing

A golfer must have the fundamentals on which to build the rest of his game. So, if he doesn't have a proper grip, he lacks one of golf's most important basics. Without a good grip he cannot expect to reach his maximum ability. Somewhere along the line his progress will stop.

Therefore, a satisfactory grip is one of the most important factors in playing good golf. The wedge should be gripped lightly—for feel—but firmly in the last three fingers of the left hand so it won't turn upon entering turf or sand.

Next to a proper grip, the way you position yourself to strike the ball will determine how well the shot is played.

I don't move the ball around in my stance. I play all shots off the left heel. The only difference is in the position of the right foot. You move it to the left on the shorter shots and back to the right on the longer shots.

As I look at the ball at address, it is an imaginary line just about two or three inches inside my left heel.

As I said, I feel that the position of the ball in relation to the left foot should be constant for most shots with all clubs.

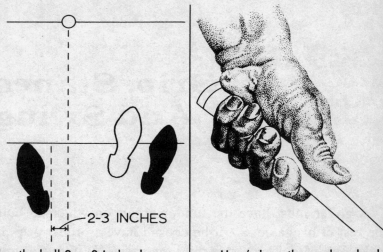

Play the ball 2 or 3 inches be-hind the left heel (dotted line area) on all conventional wedge shots.

Here's how the wedge should be gripped, with the most pres-sure on the last three fingers of the left hand.

That is, the ball should be played from slightly inside the left heel whether you are hitting a 2-iron, a wedge or even a fairway wood. The only time the ball is positioned differ-ently is on a drive (moved a bit more forward) or when you are trying to do something a little different with a shot.

Thus, the position remains constant about 90% of the time. If you start moving the ball around in relation to this specific position, it will be necessary for you to change the arc of your swing and the way you hit the ball, thus adding a number of factors and possible errors that must be con-sidered.

With the wedge, it is very easy to get the feeling that you are playing the ball back farther than is actually the case. I think what happens is that you are positioning your feet a little differently—in a more open stance—and have more of your weight to the left side. Thus, your balance is a

little different and so is the angle at which you are looking
at the ball. But the actual position should remain constant.

In playing a full wedge shot, the stance should be slightly
open. The left foot is pulled back about four inches more
than the right from an imaginary line parallel to the line of
flight. I personally feel that it is better to think of your right
foot as being placed slightly forward toward the ball. In this
way, you are better able to get the feel of keeping the left
foot in a constant position. As the shot becomes shorter, a
slightly more open stance is used—the right foot being
moved even more toward the ball.

SHIFTING WEIGHT

For a full shot with the wedge, I like to feel that I have
about 60% of my weight on my left foot at address. I then
use the same swing that I use with a 9-iron or an 8-iron or
any other club in the bag. This entails a weight shift to the
right and then back again to the left, with a full body turn.
The club is taken back the maximum distance—consistent
with control—just as with any other club. However, the
shorter club length of the wedge and the open stance automatically shorten the length of the backswing. Thus, prac-
tically all of the necessary adjustments are built right into
the club and into the way you address the ball.

As the wedge shot becomes shorter, I feel that I am
putting more and more weight on my left side at address and
shifting less to the right during the backswing. When I get
down to a ten or 15-yard pitch, I have a maximum amount
of weight on my left side (about 80%) and do not shift my
weight at all during the swing. This short shot is executed

with the arms, wrists and hands and maximum accuracy i
obtained by keeping body movement at a minimum, thu
making the swing as compact and simple as possible.

SWINGING THROUGH THE BALL

One of the most difficult concepts for the novice to believe
is that the loft of the club will get the ball airborne. A
simple a fact as this really is, there is something about the
subconscious that makes a learning golfer want to help the
ball into the air. The result, of course, is a scooping action
The player's weight remains on his right foot and the club
either cuts into the ground well behind the ball or else i
skims the ground behind the ball and tops it above center on
the upswing. If they would only realize that by hitting

CORRECT | INCORRECT

For short pitch shots, weight is on the left foot and hands are
ahead of the ball at address (*left*). "Scooping" results when
weight is on the right foot and the hands are behind the ball
(*right*). This can result in topping or scuffing.

rough the ball—or even by thinking of hitting down on
e ball—the loft of the club will do all of the lifting. Then
olfers would be well on the way to obtaining the proper
edge swing.

After sinking a pitch shot from 75 yards away, Ford kisses h
golf ball as he retrieves it from the cup in 1958 Atlanta Ope

Chapter Three

The Pitch Shot

Beginners taking up golf will find it highly profitable to learn the fundamentals of the game by starting with the short wedge shot, commonly known as the pitch shot. Practicing these short shots—from about 30 yards or less—makes the full wedge swing come easier, which in turn works into the rest of the clubs. The same swing principles hold true for all clubs.

It may be difficult for the novice to believe that with the short swing he will be able to impart enough speed or distance to the ball to get it where he wants it to go. He therefore tries to put all kinds of body action into the shot. The effects of these additional body motions are many, and they often result in sclaffing (hitting behind the ball), shanking and topping.

Probably the most important advantage of starting to play golf with the short wedge shots is that the student learns early it is best to have his weight on the left side when hitting the ball. On these shots I feel as if I'm keeping nearly 80 per cent of my weight on my left foot throughout the swing.

The stance for the pitch (*left*) has the weight to the left. There is little body movement as the golfer takes the club back (*right*).

There should be little, if any, body motion, as the short wedge shot is strictly a hand, arm and wrist action.

ADDRESS AND SWING

The address position for the pitch shot is one of ease and comfort: knees slightly bent, weight to the left, arms and hands in close, stance slightly open, ball played off instep of left foot, and the feet close together.

There is little body movement during the swing and there is a similarity between the address and the impact positions. There is no scooping action here. Hands and wrists are firm through the ball and do not begin to break until well past impact. The head remains still until the shot is well on its way, and the follow-through is short, not even as long as the backswing.

Unfortunately, the average player has a tendency to over-

The head remains still and the golfer hits down and through the ball (*left*). Follow through low and keep your head down (*right*).

use the wedge—to use it when he really shouldn't. This happens mostly around the green, when the player is up to five or ten yards from the putting surface and the pin is well into the green.

In these instances the 6-, 7-, 8-, or 9-irons should be employed to give the ball a chance to run up to the pin. The chances of getting unfortunate or unlucky bounces are much less when the angle of the ball's flight is low. Also, accuracy is generally better with a rolling shot than with a high one, providing the surface is even and consistent as it is on most greens.

Another thing to remember about the wedge is that it is designed to stop the ball quickly through backspin. This quick-stop action may leave the ball short of the hole, so a less-lofted club, which allows more run on the ball, is safer when there is plenty of green between you and the hole.

Doug Ford, the author, lines up with his 1957 Ryder Cup team-
mates. From left to right: Ford, Dick Mayer, Jack Burke, Jr., and
Lionel Hebert.

Chapter Four

High And Low
— Cut And Punch

In almost any round of golf, there are occasions when you want to use the wedge a little differently than you use it on a normal pitch shot. When you want to hit it low, the punch shot will come in handy. When you want to hit it higher than usual, the cut shot is the technique to use.

THE PUNCH SHOT

The punch shot is used mostly in a crosswind or directly into the wind when you are from 30 to 50 yards from the green. The trajectory of the shot is lower than normal, thus lessening the effect of the wind. The shot really doesn't fly with as much backspin as you might think. The ball has a sort of jumping, biting action on the green and you have to judge the amount of run very carefully.

It is vital that you keep your weight to the left side in hitting the punch shot. In fact, at address you may even be

THE PUNCH SHOT is used to keep the ball low. Your weight must be kept to the left side and the ball must be played back toward the right foot a bit. The follow-through is low.

leaning a little bit in the direction of the target with your hands well ahead of the ball (toward the target).

I prefer to play the ball from the same position on all shots, but this is one instance where it is necesary to alter your position. The ball should be played a bit more toward the right foot than normal. The stance remains open, as with the normal wedge shot.

In execution, you feel as if your hands are going through the ball lower than normal. Although the club is still descending when it meets the ball, the follow-through is low. Thus, the divot appears well ahead of the ball's original position. A firm left arm and wrists drive the club into the ball and turf. This is reflected in the finish, which is very short. At the finish of the swing you should be pointing the club just about in the direction of the flag.

THE CUT SHOT

The cut shot, which is just the opposite of the punch shot, has a high, floating trajectory. It is the shot to use when the wind is at your back and you have a bunker to clear, or under normal conditions when you must hit over a tree or a large bunker and stop the ball quickly on the green.

Instead of changing my stance in the sense of moving the ball toward the left foot, I lay back (open) the blade and open my stance more for the cut shot. This will cause the clubhead to move into the ball from outside the intended line of flight, cutting under the ball and imparting clockwise, or slice, spin to the ball. Therefore, I aim to the left of the hole, as the ball will have a left to right action when it lands. The open stance makes my backswing a little more upright, although I swing the club in exactly the same way

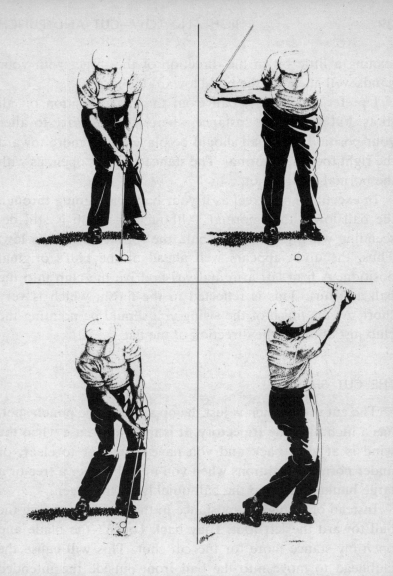

THE CUT SHOT is used to hit the ball high and/or stop it quickly. Position the ball off your left heel, open the blade and stance, and aim to the left of the hole. Hit down on the shot. The loft of the clubface will get the ball into the air.

as in a normal shot. This time, however, the follow-through is much easier and higher, the result of a free-swinging shot.

The cut shot can only be made when the ball is sitting up very high in the grass. It's not the type of shot you try off hard pan or from a tight lie, as the sole of the club may bounce into the ball and a skulled or topped shot may result.

Ford hits a trap shot in the sudden death playoff of the 1962
Crosby Invitational at Pebble Beach, Calif. The ball stopped
six feet from the cup. Ford won over Joe Campbell.

Chapter Five

Trouble? Wedge!

If I were playing a word-association game and someone said "trouble" my answer would probably be "wedge," for the pitching wedge and sand wedge have helped me escape from more trouble than all of the other clubs combined.

The wedge is such a great trouble club because of its extra weight and extreme loft. The weight helps send the clubhead through the rough or sand and the loft clears the ball into the air quickly.

I attribute my win in the 1962 Crosby Invitational tournament to being able to use the wedge effectively in a difficult situation. On the par-5 18th I drove my second shot with a spoon into an old divot hole. I was standing below the ball and shooting into a cross-wind. It was about a 65-to-75-yard shot. I had to compensate for all these factors: soft, wet turf; digging the ball out of the tight lie; standing below the ball, and the strong crosswind. In this case I addressed the ball back toward my right foot a little, hooded the blade and made a very sharp descending blow on the ball. It came out low as if I had hit it with a 4-iron. The ball hit the green with a lot of backspin. The green was wet and the ball pulled up pretty good. I was able to two-putt and make a par, whereas I really didn't think I'd be able to get on the green at all from the position. That tied me with Joe Campbell at 286 for 72 holes. I was lucky enough to win the sudden-death playoff on the first extra hole and pocketed the first place check of $5,300. Joe took home $3,400.

Incidentally, it was my sand wedge that helped me win the playoff. I came out of a trap to within six feet of the hole and sank the putt for a par while Campbell was three-putting from the front edge of the green.

One important thing to remember about the use of the wedge is that the type of lie, in most cases, dictates the type of shot you have to play. But your main concern should *ALWAYS* be to get the ball on the green. *Think!* KNOW what you can do. Don't try any trick shots that aren't likely to come off.

So far, this book has covered the basic full wedge shot, the short approach, or pitch, the punch shot and the cut shot. Putting these shots to use under different and varying circumstances requires a lot of experience. Although many situations arise that are similar to others encountered before, no two shots are ever really exactly alike in every detail. That is why it is important to practice so much with the wedge, under as wide a variety of situations as possible.

PLAYING FROM THE ROUGH

One of the most common trouble shots where the wedge is indispensable is from the taller grass that borders fairways.

On many courses, this "rough" is so short that it hardly does justice to the term. On others, the grass may extend in length all the way up to the spinach they called rough in the 1958 U.S. Open at Southern Hills C.C. in Tulsa.

This was Bermuda grass that had been fertilized, watered and permitted to grow as high as eight to ten inches in length. It was so lush it would fall over the ball so you could hardly see it. This was the worst stuff to play out of I have ever seen. The only thing we could do was to use the wedge to get the ball back into the fairway where we would try to make a great recovery shot. There was no way you could get distance on the ball if you got in that rough.

Tommy Bolt won the U.S. Open that year and his 72-hole total of 283 was such a great performance that nobody came within four strokes of it. Gary Player was second at 287 and Julius Boros third at 289. Yours truly had one of his worst totals ever—301. Arnold Palmer had 299.

In playing out of short rough, such as that normally found just off the fairway and sometimes around the outer fringes of the green, we are really not talking about a "trouble" shot. From short rough you might still be able to use the normal club for the particular length of the shot.

Yet even from short rough, when the blade of the wedge —or any other club—comes into the grass before contacting the ball, the grass will tend to wrap itself around the clubhead. This closes the blade at impact. To compensate for this tendency, which varies greatly depending on the strength and length of the grass, I just cock the blade a little open at address and thus have it a bit open at impact.

This opening of the face is especially necessary for a high shot from rough when I want as little roll as possible on the ball after it lands. As for the actual execution of the shot, it is played as a normal full wedge or short wedge pitch. On the short shot, it is vital to grip the club firmly and hit the ball crisply. This is important on all shots, of course, but it is of double importance in hitting from the rough.

As the wedge enters rough, heavy grass will wrap around the hosel, retarding the heel and causing the clubface to close. To compensate, open the blade at address.

If distance is required on the shot from rough, I might not open the face at address. I will probably hood, or close, the clubface a little with the hands ahead of the ball and aim a bit right of the target. The ball will then come out with a hook spin and roll farther than normal, adding distance to the shot.

One thing you must remember is that the amount of backspin you can get is minimized in direct proportion to the amount of grass between the clubface and ball at impact and by the amount of gripping action the grass in front of the ball will have on the ball as it comes out.

Another factor that often comes into play is the direction in which the grass happens to be lying, that is, against the shot or with it—or across it. When the grass is against the shot it is important to contact as little grass as possible before the clubhead hits the ball. This is done by playing the

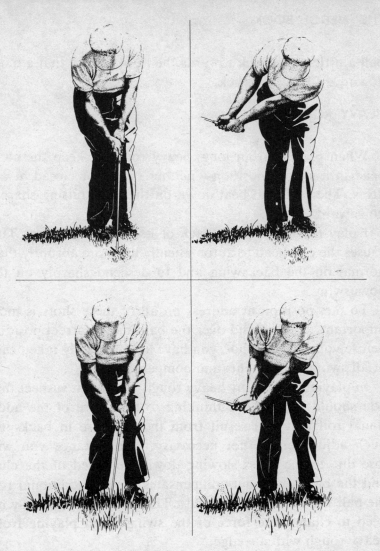

Compare the stroke on a normal pitch shot (*top*) to a shot made from heavy rough (*bottom*). From heavy rough, play the ball slightly back of the normal position. This causes you to lift the clubhead more abruptly on your backswing and leads to a sharper downward stroke.

ball a little more back towards the right foot so that a more downward blow is struck.

HEAVY ROUGH

When playing from long, heavy rough, I keep the clubhead in a square position—neither open nor closed at address. Then I try to beat down on the shot, hitting sharply downward.

I play the ball slightly back of its normal position. This causes the clubhead to automatically lift more abruptly than normal on the backswing and to descend sharply on the downswing.

To me, position at address on all of these shots is most important. If you stand over the ball in the correct position before you start the shot, you have automatically taken care of all swing adjustments and compensations.

In playing out of any heavy rough you might suspect that you should adjust your thinking to take care of the additional roll that will result from the decrease in backspin. Such adjustment is not necessary. The distance you will lose due to the grass slowing down the speed of the club and the ball just about compensates for the additional roll the ball will have when it lands. Therefore there is really no need to change the force of the swing when playing from heavy rough with a wedge.

REVIEW—HITTING FROM THE ROUGH

To review, here are the fundamentals you should remember when playing a wedge from the rough:

1. Remember that the club should come into contact with the grass before it reaches the ball. Cock the blade a little open at address to allow for the tendency of the grass to close the clubface.
2. Grip the club firmly and hit the ball crisply.
3. Estimate the distance required, allowing for backspin and more roll.
4. In heavy rough, play the ball slightly back of the normal position. This will cause a sharper downswing.

Blasting out of water, Ford makes a big splash on 15th hole in the 1957 Masters tournament at Augusta, Ga. A 66 in the final round made him the Masters champion that year.

Chapter Six

More Trouble Shots

The game of golf is a great challenge because you never know where or how your ball will end up. The next shot you encounter quite possibly will be like no other shot you've ever had before. It may be similar, but the exact circumstances will probably vary.

What the average golfer might consider a difficult shot is only difficult when he doesn't know how to handle it. A little knowledge, a good wedge and keeping the old "noggin" down will often make a tough shot come off with ease.

Let's discuss some more trouble shots and how to handle them like a pro.

CLOSE LIE

A close or tight lie is one where the ball lies on a bare spot. It might even be in a divot mark or on some ground where the grass has been worn away. In other words it is a lie from which, if you hit a little behind the ball, you will catch the ground and not the grass in which the ball would be sitting in a normal lie. A close lie allows little, if any, margin for error.

In these situations, it is imperative that you hit the ball before contacting the ground. That is the primary consideration. One aid in doing this is to position yourself so your hands are a bit more forward (toward the target) at the address position. Then bend your right arm sharply on the backswing, keeping your right elbow close to your side. In this way, you are leading the shot more and will help insure contacting the ball first.

The pitching wedge, with its extra weight, will ride along freely below the surface of the turf. It is an ideal club for tight lies where you must cut through the ground without losing much clubhead speed. Be sure you stroke the ball firmly to insure a solid, crisp hit.

HARD PAN

Hard pan is solid, baked ground that could be likened to a sidewalk or a roadway. It is probably the worst possible lie from which to use the wedge, because on a missed shot the design of the club's sole will cause it to bounce into the ball. A "sculled" shot results, where the club meets the ball on the upswing and produces a low, uncontrolled, driving shot. From hard pan, it is usually smarter to use a club without such a definitely flanged sole—one that will cut under the ball instead of bouncing. Then, if the shot is slightly missed, it still has a chance.

If it is absolutely necessary to use the wedge, because you must carry over an obstacle, again take an upright back-

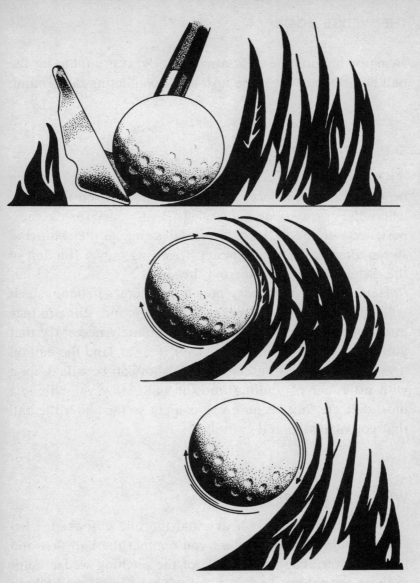

Tall grass will grip the ball as it is hit out, thus minimizing the amount of backspin you will get. You can expect a shot from tall grass to roll far after it lands.

swing by hinging the right arm abruptly. It is vital to hit the ball before, or at the same instant, as contacting the ground.

BALL SITTING UP

One situation that can be a real fooler finds the ball sitting up rather high in short stubby rough or even on a fairway where the grass is long and stiff. It is very easy for the inexperienced golfer to take a normal swing at the ball and sweep almost completely under it, getting only a fraction of the distance he expected from the shot.

Here is where the wedge punch shot comes in handy, as it will permit you to hit the ball squarely and still produce much backspin. Of course, if it is absolutely necessary that you hit a very high shot, to go over trees or land the ball on a very small piece of green, the cut shot can be called upon with little fear of sculling into the ball. However, this is a most delicate shot because you can cut so far under the ball that you almost miss it entirely.

WET, SOGGY TURF

When the weather is heavy and the turf is soaked it becomes doubly important that you contact the ball first and the turf after. The flanged sole of the pitching wedge helps in these conditions. In fact, if I don't have to hit the ball too far off of soggy turf, I will often use the sand wedge just to get the advantage of the additional "ride" that is built into the sole, which prevents the club from digging too deeply.

Even so, it is important not to contact the ground prior

to meeting the ball, and a good follow-through will help the shot come off as desired. The shot is very similar to hitting off of wet sand, which will be covered later in the book. The flanged sole helps you get the clubhead through the ball and turf with sufficient speed and without digging too deeply.

The moisture will reduce the ball-club friction which, in turn, minimizes effective backspin on the shot. You can expect the ball to roll considerably when it lands unless the green is also soggy.

PLUGGED LIE

If you are unfortunate enough to encounter a plugged lie (ball buried or semi-buried in turf), you must realize that you are not going to get much distance from the shot. Usually, you are lucky to get the ball out of the hole and back into play.

The wedge shot from such a lie is played like a semi-explosion shot from sand. I hood the blade a little so that it faces left of target and hit somewhere between an eighth of an inch to a half inch behind the ball, depending on how deeply it is buried. The deeper it's buried, the farther back you must hit in order to keep from cutting into the top of the ball. The player must figure how he can get the leading edge of the club below the equator of the ball.

The extra weight of the wedge comes in handy on this shot, and the loft of the club should pop the ball out and back into play.

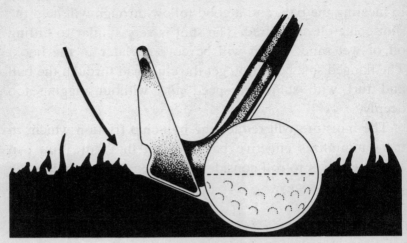

If a plugged ball is contacted just below its "equator," it will pop out of the hole. Your swing will lose power if you try to ram the clubhead too deeply into the ground.

THE WEDGE IN THE WIND

More than any other time, playing the wedge in the wind requires a sound knowledge of spin and how the ball reacts under various circumstances. The wind also makes it most difficult to keep one's balance and to hit shots with a normal swing.

Crosswind—This shot is undoubtedly the most difficult of conditions in which to use the wedge. In fact I will rarely, if ever, play any kind of a full-wedge shot in a crosswind. I prefer to take a nine-iron, maybe choking down on it a bit to get a lower trajectory with more control.

The high trajectory of the wedge shot permits the wind to affect it more than any other shot. With a 25 to 30 mile an hour crosswind you will actually lose about one-third of the actual flight distance of the ball, and the shot can be thrown off direction as much as 10 to 15 yards.

Against the Wind—The wedge is a very effective club to use against the wind if you can properly judge the distance you must hit the shot. You must make up your mind that you have to fly the ball all the way to the pin—or even beyond—because the chances are that the ball will be backing up a bit just before it lands. You must also realize on this shot that the ball will most likely go higher than usual due to the greater effectiveness of the backspin. Thus the wind will act on the ball for a longer period of time and shorten the effective distance of the shot even more. The punch shot is usually best into wind because it flies lower than normal.

With the Wind—When the wind is with you, one thing to watch out for is the overspin the ball will pick up when it lands. The ball will be coming into the green with more forward thrust and speed than normal, thus reducing the effect of the backspin and adding considerably to the roll. A soft cut shot will help minimize this forward thrust.

The wedge is a club that can make the difference between a mediocre round of golf and a good one. The instruction presented in this chapter on the various trouble shots that can be encountered in your short game are those that are common among professionals and amateurs alike. Your ability to use this instruction effectively will be determined by your own knowledge of what you can do with the pitching wedge.

Practice, therefore, becomes an important factor. I cannot stress too much the importance of becoming familiar with your wedge. It is to your advantage to simulate every possible lie—both good and bad—and practice until you have reached a degree of skill with which you are satisfied.

This, then, is the pitching wedge. From this point on we

The "bounce" or "ride" in a wedge keeps the clubhead from digging deeply into the ground when a descending blow is struck (*top*). The flanged sole makes the club "ride" below the surface without digging as deeply as would the straighter-faced 9-iron (*bottom*).

will discuss the sand wedge. But remember what you have already learned. As you become more and more proficient in the use of the pitching wedge, you will find that you will turn to it more and more, as do all of the successful professional golfers of today.

Ford blasts from a sand trap on his way to victory in the 1955 PGA championship at Northville, Michigan.

Chapter Seven

The Right Sand Wedge For You

Many amateurs fear the sand trap shot although it is one of the easiest, most routine shots in golf.

If you know the proper technique, there is nothing difficult about exploding from sand. But if you fear the shot, you have two strikes against you. Confidence and a little knowledge is all it takes to pop the ball out of the trap and onto the green, time after time.

After a while, you can get so you're blasting the ball up within one-putt range.

Paul Runyan, the famous golf teacher, has said, "I would prefer to have my ball 40 feet away from the hole in an ordinary sand trap lie than behind a bunker on good grass 90 feet away. Also, I would rather have a short explosion shot of 25 feet than a putt of 60 feet."

This is the way most pros feel. There are many times when I will aim right for the pin even if it is tucked close to a bunker. I'd rather land in the trap, close to the pin, than on the other side of the green where I might have a long putt over a lot of undulations.

Confidence is important. Not only in the sand shot, but in your putting stroke. If you feel sure you can knock in those six and eight foot putts, it will make you more confident that you can get down in two from a sand trap. After a while, you'll find yourself blasting to within two or three feet of the pin. It just takes a good wedge, a little learning and confidence.

THE RIGHT SAND WEDGE

The importance of having the correct "tools" for sand play was brought home to me at the very beginning of my career as a touring professional. Lloyd Mangrum pointed out that the sand wedge I had been using as an amateur would not produce top results. My club was built more like a pitching wedge than a sand wedge in that it had little "ride" in the sole. In other words, the back point of the sole line dipped only slightly below the horizontal as compared to the leading edge.

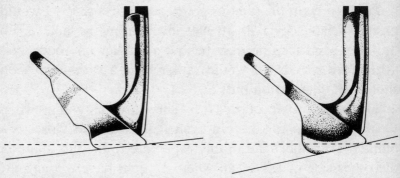

The amount of clubhead's sole falling below the horizontal is called "ride." Sand wedges (right) have more ride than pitching wedges (left).

Using this club, I was taking too much sand on my trap shots and was unable to control the ball well enough to score in the professional range. Taking Mangrum's advice, I obtained a sand wedge with more ride and immediately noticed an improvement in my sand play.

The sand wedge I have been using for the past 14 years has a "rocker" or slightly rounded sole which isn't too wide. Many of the sand wedges being marketed today have too much area between the leading and the trailing edges of the sole. Such soles provide to much ride. They will not take enough sand and the clubhead will not ride smoothly under the ball. A golfer takes the chance of getting too much of the ball and flying it farther than desired.

My sand wedge is versatile enough to use in most types of sand, although for some years I have thought of using different kinds of wedges for different varieties of sand. For instance, in the fluffy, loose sand at Tulsa's Southern Hills C.C. during the 1958 U. S. Open, a club with a more steeply-inclined sole would have been the one to use. The sand was so loose you needed a club which would ride as close to the surface as possible. A deep-digging sand wedge simply wouldn't move the ball as far as desired.

A golfer who has the proper sand wedge does not have to make any alterations in his normal pitching wedge or 9-iron swing to execute a sand shot. Golfers who start thinking about different swings for sand shots are bound to become confused. They'll loose the concentration they dearly need to make this shot successful.

When you're in a sand trap, you are there only because you have misplayed a previous shot. Try not to let this upset you and concentrate only on getting the ball as close as possible to the hole. If you have a good sand wedge and a constant and uncomplicated sand trap swing, your chances of getting down in two are increased.

ANIMATED INSTRUCTION SECTION

Featuring Flip-Vision, Doug Ford is shown performing the basic fairway wedge shot (page 65 to 95) and the basic sand wedge shot (page 97 to 127). By "flipping" the pages in this section, you can follow, in sequence, *the full motion of each swing from address to follow-through.* The accompanying instruction block with each illustration describes the important factors shown at that particular point of the swing.

Stance is slightly open
at address.

Club is taken away
low to the ground.

Body does not sway.
Shoulders tilt and turn.

Left arm is straight dur-
ing backswing which is
short and crisp, not
long and lazy.

Weight shifts to the left
as the downswing be-
gins.

Now pull down with the left arm, keeping your eyes glued on the ball.

Note position of the hands as if driving the grip end of the club into the ground.

Uncocking of wrists
has been delayed until
now.

Left hip has been turned and is "out of the way."

Arms bring the hands into hitting position smoothly.

Stay down on the shot, so that the clubhead will hit the ball before the ground.

At impact, the club-
head is moving down
and through the ball.

Head stays down after impact so that the swing stays in the groove.

At impact and following, the right arm straightens.

Note that the head is still down. Anxious "looking up" will cause flubbed shots.

Balance is retained on
full follow-through.

Start with your weight
on the left side. Don't
"sole" the club.

Weight shifts to the right. Body turns—does not sway.

Note the straight left arm on backswing.

Begin downswing by returning your weight to the left side.

Pull down with the left
arm.

Right elbow has re-
turned to the right
side.

Uncocking of wrists
has been delayed until
now.

Hands continue to lead
the open clubface.

Constant firm grip is kept throughout the stroke.

Aim to strike sand about one inch behind the ball.

Flick through the sand
with hands and wrists.

Clubhead shouldn't touch ball. Blasted sand propels it to the green.

Keep clubhead moving
toward target.

Don't quit at this point.
Continue the swing.

Head has been kept
steady until this point.

Use a full follow-through on every sand shot.

The Basic Sand Shot

Now let us discuss the basic sand shot, the shot used from a good lie in dry sand when no unusual amount of height or distance is required.

STANCE, AIM AND SWING

The stance for the basic sand shot should be more open than on fairway wedge shots, the right foot closer than the left to the intended line of flight. This will automatically produce swing-arc changes designed to put more backspin on the ball. The ball should be positioned on a line extending from slightly inside the left heel.

A more open stance shortens the length of the backswing. You don't have to think about this. It happens automatically since the open stance restricts the hip and shoulder turn on the backswing.

The open stance also causes the clubhead to move slightly outside its normal path on the backswing and to slice across

the ball at impact. This puts a left-to-right spin on the ball
When the ball hits, it will tend to turn to the right. Thus,
usually aim to a spot about two feet to the left of the hole.

On long sand shots—50 feet or more—the ball will have
more backspin than on shorter shots. Therefore, I aim more
directly at the pin, since the backspinning ball will not run
very far and will not have a chance to bounce and roll so
far to the right.

There should be very little body action in the sand shot
swing—just enough to instill rhythm. I prefer to think that
the open stance and resulting lack of turn causes my body—
including the head—to remain almost motionless throughout the shot. The swing is mostly with the hands, arms and
wrists.

POINT OF ENTRY AND FOLLOWING-THROUGH

On every normal sand shot, long or short, I plan for the
clubhead to hit the sand about one inch behind the ball. It is
a fairly direct hit at the sand, as the open stance makes the
backswing more abrupt and upright than on a normal fairway shot. I regulate the distance I need by adjusting the
amount of power I put into the swing. This, to an extent,
revolves around the length of the backswing. However, good
sand players merely concentrate on the power needed. The
backswing will automatically adjust to whatever length is
necessary.

For instance, if the pin is fairly close to the near edge of
the green, I will be conscious of the fact that I do not want
to hit the ball very far. A "sixth sense" will thus shorten the
backswing, because I know I don't need as much power.

Adjusting the amount the stance is open will also help

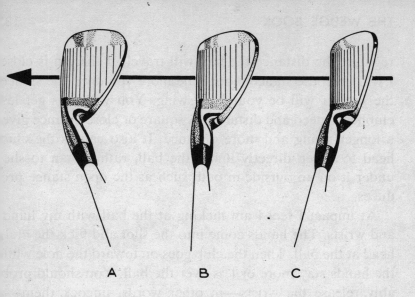

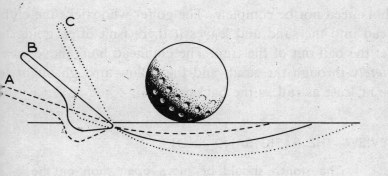

The more you lay back (open) the clubface on a sand shot, the less sand you will take and the farther the ball will fly. Note how open (A), square (B) and closed (C) faces, shown in upper drawings as they look to the golfer, take varying amounts of and from under the ball (*approximate paths of clubheads are shown by dotted lines in drawing below*).

regulate the distance the ball will travel. If the pin is close
I will open the stance more. The more you open the stance
the shorter will be your backswing. You will thus get les
clubhead speed and distance. A square or closed stance give
a longer swing and more distance. It also causes the clut
head to sweep directly under the ball, rather than to slic
under it on an outside-in path such as the open stance pro
duces.

At impact I feel I am flicking at the ball with my hand
and wrists. The hands come into the shot and flick the clut
head at the ball. Then the club goes on toward the hole whil
the hands stay more or less over the ball. You should prot
ably release the wrists—in other words, uncock them—,
little earlier than on a normal fairway shot.

This flicking should not lead anyone to believe that sand
shots need not be complete. The golfer who sticks the clut
head into the sand and leaves it there isn't often going to
get the ball out of the trap. The clubhead must move com
pletely through the sand, and the follow-through ought to
be at least as full as the backswing.

REVIEW—THE BASIC SAND SHOT

1. The stance should be more open than on the
   fairway wedge shot with the right foot closer than
   the left to the intended line of flight.
2. A long sand shot will have more backspin than
   a short shot. Aim about two feet left of the pin
   because the open stance will tend to put a left-to-
   right spin on the ball when it hits the green.
3. Keep the body movement to a minimum—just
   enough to instill rhythm.

4. Under normal conditions, plan for the clubhead to hit the sand about one inch behind the ball.

5. Release your wrists slightly earlier than on a normal fairway shot so that at impact you feel you are flicking at the ball with your hands and wrists.

6. Most important—follow through on all sand shots!

Knowing how to play out of sand leads to lower scores. Here
Ford masters a trap in the Insurance City Open at Hartford,
Conn.

Chapter Nine

Sand, Sand
Everywhere

Touring professionals out of necessity become familiar with just about every possible type of sand trap and sand shot. Rarely do we run into the same kind of sand two weeks in a row, and certainly the varieties of shots we must make are almost uncountable.

The weekend golfer usually becomes closely acquainted with only a few types of sand, since most of his play is in his own locality and ordinarily on only one or two courses. However, he must contend with the same wide spectrum of shots from such sand as do the playing professionals.

Unless you play frequently in different parts of the country, I recommend that you concentrate on learning the proper techniques for getting out of the particular type of sand at your course and at courses in your area.

TYPES OF SAND

"Coast" sand—Coastal courses have the simplest kind of

sand from which to escape. The base of these traps is packed with only a quarter or a half inch of loose sand on top. This firm base makes it possible to play consistently good sand shots and with greater ease because it keeps the clubhead from digging. The leading edge of the wedge may enter the sand quite close to the ball. The solid base offers strong resistance to the clubhead, much the same as turf on the fairway. A well-played ball from this sand will have plenty of "stop" or backspin.

Nevertheless, the wedge should enter the sand behind the ball—less than an inch for the ordinary shot from coastal sand. Since coastal sand does have this resistant base, it is important to make sure that the clubhead cuts well under the ball. Use a square or only slightly laid back (opened) clubface to achieve this result.

As a general rule for all sand shots, the more the blade is laid back (or opened so that the clubface would point to the right of the target if the stance were not adjusted), the higher the clubhead will ride through the sand; the more the face is closed to the target (or hooded), the deeper the club head will dig.

"Dirt" sand—Inland courses generally feature what is known as "dirt" sand. It probably has more individual variations than any other type of sand. Usually coarse, it can have imperfections such as actual chunks of semi-solid dirt or sand. Touchy lies frequently occur.

Inland sand often has a looser texture than coastal sand and the wedge can penetrate it more easily. Therefore, lay back (open) the face a bit more than normal so the club head will ride closer to the surface of the sand. A deeper undercut may leave the ball in the trap.

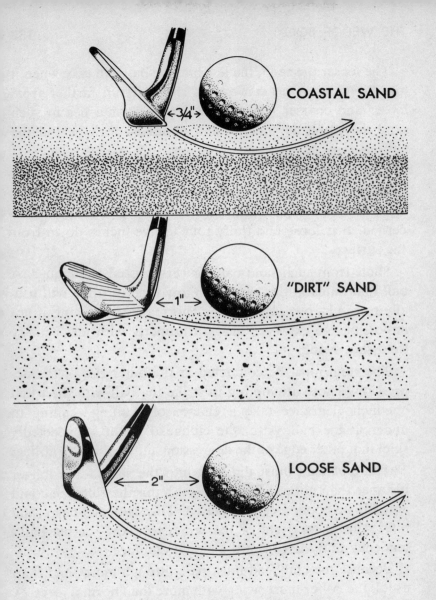

COASTAL SAND

←3/4"→

"DIRT" SAND

←1"→

LOOSE SAND

←2"→

The position of the clubhead and where it enters the sand varies when playing out of different types of sand.

The looser the sand, the less bite the ball will take when it hits the green. One can expect shots to run farther from looser and coarser inland sand. From normal lies in such sand the clubhead should enter about an inch behind the ball.

Loose sand—Occasionally we find traps filled with extremely loose "ersatz" sand, sometimes called silica sand. This sand has no base at all as far as the golf swing is concerned. It is loose and fluffy four to five inches down from the surface.

Shots from such sand call for very special techniques. A ball that lands in this sand with any kind of force will usually rest in its own depression. This makes it difficult, if not impossible, to extricate the ball properly with an ordinary sand shot swing.

The sand must be contacted at the outer rim of the depression. Those attempting to strike the ball with the usual one-inch clearance take a chance of skulling—failing to undercut the ball. Also, the clubhead might unexpectedly skim that outer edge of the depression and be thrown off-line.

The clubhead must dig well into the sand for a longer distance than normal. To accomplish this the clubface could actually be hooded (closed) a bit. This assures a deep sand bite. Aim to the right of the target to allow for the ball's tendency to fly left from the closed clubface.

Because the clubhead must pass through more sand than usual, the golfer must swing with more than normal force. A ball struck from this type of sand will tend to be "dead"—lacking backspin—and will run upon hitting the green's surface.

The Rules of Golf prohibit testing sand texture. But, by

planting your feet to get a firm stance (which is within the rules), you can get an indication of how much loose sand there is on the surface and how firm is the base.

Time spent practicing sand shots can save strokes on the course. Here, Doug Ford works out in a practice sand trap and attracts admiring spectators.

Chapter Ten

Trouble Shots From Sand

UPHILL LIE

One of the toughest sand shots is the one made from an uphill lie because the clubhead encounters more sand resistance than usual. Since the clubhead must pass through a greater volume of sand, it is best to swing harder than usual and to concentrate on a full follow-through.

The ball should be played well forward in the stance—opposite the left foot—just as you would from an uphill lie in the fairway. The steeper the slant, the farther forward (toward the target) the ball should appear in the stance.

An extremely deep penetration of the clubhead into the sand is not desirable. So lay back (open) the clubface at address. This will keep the sole of the clubhead closer to the surface of the sand. The clubhead should strike the sand an inch or less behind the ball to minimize the amount of sand it must encounter.

The ball will rise rapidly in a steep trajectory and will not roll much after it lands.

This is just about the type of shot I holed on the 72nd green of the 1957 Masters. This was the last of 66 strokes in that round, which still stands as a fourth-round Masters record, and it helped me win the tournament. Actually, my ball was buried a bit and, to be sure I got well under it, I kept the clubface just about normal instead of laid back.

DOWNHILL LIE

The opposite of the uphill lie, the problem in this case is to move the clubhead through enough sand that it cuts under the ball. The clubface should be hooded (closed) a bit so it will dig deeply into the sand. The ball should be played more toward the right foot, as on an ordinary downhill fairway shot. Aim to hit slightly farther (say two inches) behind the ball.

This is a rugged shot because the ball will fly low and with hardly any backspin. It's the sort of shot that even good players occasionally skull across the green and into a trap on the other side. So be careful to cut under the ball.

There are circumstances that permit another approach to this shot. I once saw Ed Furgol pull out of a nasty situation that involved a steep, downhill sand lie by using the 3-iron. There was no way he could get the ball up quickly enough so it would stop near the pin. So Furgol played the shot with the 3-iron, actually running the ball down and over the surface of the sand, up the side of the bunker (there was no lip, of course) and on to the green. It was a great shot—one that can be extremely handy.

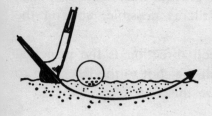

NORMAL

1. Clubface laid back (opened) slightly.
2. Ball played on line slightly inside left heel.
3. Clubhead enters sand one inch behind ball.

UPHILL

1. Clubface laid back (opened) slightly.
2. Ball played on line opposite left toes.
3. Clubhead enters sand one inch or less behind ball.

DOWNHILL

1. Clubface hooded (closed) slightly.
2. Ball is played farther back (toward center of stance) than normal.
3. Clubhead enters sand two inches behind ball.

SIDEHILL LIE

Not an easy shot, especially when the ball is below the feet. Most people, including myself, grip the club down two or three inches from the butt end on sand shots. This gives a feeling of maximum security and control. However, when the ball is below the feet, the club must be lengthened by gripping it nearer the end. The great danger is raising the whole body at impact and topping or skulling the shot. A "longer" grip helps prevent this. Make a special effort to keep the body as still as possible, and on the same level.

With the ball above the feet, direction is the principal danger. The tendency is to pull the shot to the left. Aim to the right of the pin to minimize this.

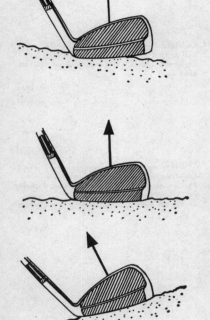

BALL BELOW FEET
(Arrow indicates line of flight)
1. Take grip on end of shaft.
2. Clubface squared to line of flight.
3. Clubhead enters sand one inch behind ball.
4. Stay "down" on shot until finish.

BALL ABOVE FEET
Upper drawing indicates how normal sand shot would look from behind. Lower drawing shows how normal stance, clubface angle and swing would hit ball to left of target. Therefore:
1. Aim slightly to the right of the target.
2. Clubface laid back (opened) slightly.
3. Grip down on club to accommodate fact that ball is closer to the hands.
4. Ball played on line slightly inside left heel.
5. Clubhead enters sand one inch behind ball.

WET SAND

This is probably the easiest of all sand shots, as long as the sand isn't actually mushy. The only difference between this and a regular sand shot is that you must hit the ball a little harder because the sand offers more resistance to the clubhead.

The clubface should be laid back a bit for a wet sand shot from a good lie. If it is buried, then square up or even hood (close) the clubface so the clubhead will dig more deeply into the sand and cut under the ball. Remember, you must swing with more determination than ever if you are to move a buried ball out of wet sand.

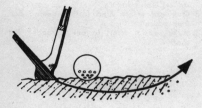

WET SAND
1. Clubface laid back (opened) slightly if ball normally situated. If buried at all clubface may be squared or even hooded (closed).
2. Ball played on line slightly inside left heel.
3. Clubhead enters sand one inch behind ball.
4. Swing harder than for normal shot.

BURIED LIE

This is a tough shot, but not impossible. The major points are to hood the clubface to facilitate a deep clubhead path into the sand and under the ball, and to hit far enough behind the ball so the clubhead has space enough to do its digging.

BURIED
1. Clubface hooded (closed) slightly.
2. Ball played farther back (toward center of stance) than normal.
3. Clubhead enters sand farther behind ball than normal.
4. Make special effort to get "through" the shot.

PLUGGED LIE

Plugged lies can be especially bothersome. This is the type of lie in which the ball goes straight down into fairly firm sand. There is very little splattering of the sand as in the "fried egg" lie which will be explained next. The ball, you might say, is at the bottom of a miniature well and might be entirely below the surface.

Give yourself plenty of room behind the ball so the club-head can cut down and under.

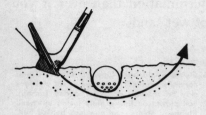

PLUGGED
1. Clubface hooded (closed) slightly.
2. Ball played farther back (toward center of stance) than normal.
3. Clubhead enters sand farther behind ball than normal.
4. Make special effort to get "through" the shot.

"FRIED EGG" LIE

This was described earlier in conjunction with the loose "ersatz" sand. The "fried egg" is encountered when the ball spatters the sand, creates a shallow, platter-like depression and comes to rest in its center.

Plan to hit three or four inches behind the ball with a squared or slightly hooded (closed) clubface, so the club-head will dip well under the ball. Put enough power in your swing to get the clubhead well "through" the sand.

'FRIED EGG'
1. Clubface hooded (closed) slightly.
2. Ball played farther back (toward center of stance) than normal.
3. Clubhead enters sand on outer rim of depression made by ball.
4. Make special effort to get "through" the shot.

CHIPPING AND PUTTING FROM SAND

These techniques are often useful and certainly advis-able if certain conditions exist. In both cases, the sand must be fairly hard, wet or baked. For putting, there must be no lip on the green side of the trap that would stop a rolling ball. And the lie must be good. Don't putt or chip from even a slightly buried lie.

If the pin is close, and the other favorable conditions exist, I will use a putter. If the pin is farther away, the chip is the best shot. But never putt or chip from sand unless you have practiced such a shot.

The principal difference between these shots and the regular sand shot is that you must hit the ball first. Should a chip be the shot, I recommend the club with the least amount of loft to get the ball out of the trap, but not straighter faced than a 6-iron. This gives better control and less chance for a flubbed shot.

Though I follow the sand shot technique outlined in this book, there are a number of professional players who depart from these precepts and still do quite well. Bill Casper, for instance, uses very little backswing and seems to chip the

PUTTING
1. Use putter only when there is no lip on the sand trap; ball is on top of sand, and hole is reasonably close to near edge of green.
2. Ball played on line slightly inside left heel.
3. Make sure clubhead strikes ball first.

CHIPPING
1. Use a 6-, 7-, 8-, or 9-iron.
2. Chip only when there is no lip on the sand trap; ball rests high on the sand, hole is not close to the near edge of the green.
4. Ball played on line slightly inside left heel.
5. Make sure clubhead strikes ball first.

ball out of the sand with a punch-like swing. Bill is especially effective on the Western courses where the bunkers don't seem to be lipped as much.

Arnold Palmer lays back (opens) the clubface on nearly all his sand shots. He does this even with "fried egg" and semi-buried shots. Arnie says he just digs it in and lets the ball pop out. But he is so strong he can do this while other players can't.

Despite the success with which these prominent players deviate from the norm in sand shots, the average player should not attempt to copy them. The points explained in this book are designed to fit the majority of golfers.

Never neglect practicing your wedges, neither the pitching wedge nor sand wedge. These are your "scoring" clubs, the sticks you must learn to use effectively to place the ball consistently on the green within one-putt distance. They also are the weapons you can use most effectively to recover from trouble.

Chapter Eleven

Be A Tiger!

Talking about hitting good wedge shots and actually going out on the course and hitting them are two different things. All the knowledge in the world won't do you much good unless you can apply it.

I'm not underrating the theory of the wedge shot or any other part of the game. That's what most of this book has been so far—theory. But golf goes farther than that. To score well, you must be a good competitor. You must hit that ball at the hole and, especially when using the wedge, as close to the hole as possible every time. You need the kind of desire that won't be quenched when you hit a wedge shot to within ten feet of the cup. The next time knock it up there within five feet.

I highly recommend that you develop sound fundamentals and build as solid and fine a golf swing as you possibly can. But I also strongly suggest that you develop a "get tough" attitude toward the game. I mean, "get tough" inwardly. Be a perfect gentleman and sportsman on the outside, but be a

Doug Ford is famous for his competitive spirit and determination—a "tiger" on the course. Here, he smashes a shot to the first green in the 1962 Masters tournament.

fighter on the inside. When you're pitching to a green, don't ask yourself:

"Will I be able to get close to the pin? Or will I flub this shot and land in that sand trap between me and the green?"

Get tough. Tell yourself:

"I'm going to smack this little apple right up there next to the cup."

If there is any doubt in your mind, you probably will swing with doubt. You might rush the takeaway, you might look up, you might quit on the shot and not follow through crisply.

If you develop a confident attitude, you'll take the club away smoothly and deliberately, keep your head down, and swing smartly through the ball. Your attitude will be reflected in your swing. If you get tough with yourself— be a tiger—you'll be tough to beat.

Many good golfers who didn't have the best swings in the world have made up for it by being the best competitors. You can't beat the combination of a good swing and a good competitor. And if there is any part of the game of golf where touch, feel and positive attitude can compensate for a less-than-perfect swing, it's in the short game. Once you're in scoring range, get that ball in the hole in as few strokes as possible. It isn't "how" that counts, it's "how many."

How often have you heard the sad story of a fine swinger who reported that he hit 15 or 16 greens in regulation but took 39 putts on the 18 greens and wound up with a 78 instead of the 72 he might have had? Or the guy who took three or four strokes to get down every time he got within wedge distance of the green, thus adding five or ten strokes to his score?

You probably have watched fellows like Arnold Palmer or Jack Nicklaus on television or in person. They have effective golf swings but the thing that must have impressed you most is that they are two great competitors—more than just golfers who have mastered the fundamentals. They also are more than just long hitters. They have tremendous desire, dynamic wills to win and brilliant short games—because they're "tigers." As somebody once said, "when the going gets tough, the tough get going."

That's a big reason why Arnold and Jack have been winning so many touranments and so much money. Yes, they're long hitters, but their great competitive drive also helps separate them from the many other excellent professionals on the tournament circuit.

WARM UP WITH THE WEDGE

When warming up for a round I suggest that a golfer hit wedge shots if he doesn't have time for anything else. You can't beat practicing with a wedge. Two or three pitch shots and two or three bunker shots will give you a feel of hand position and enable you to grasp your timing much quicker than anything else. I'd rather hit six bunker shots than ten drivers before going out to play.

Then, once on the course, don't experiment with your swing. Just hit one shot at a time, to the best of your ability, and concentrate on getting the ball in the hole in as few strokes as possible. You should improve your swing on the practice range but, on the course, you should only worry about improving your score.

By all means, don't look back and don't look too far ahead. A double bogey on the previous hole can't be erased.

And, when you're standing in the fairway getting ready to hit your wedge to the green, don't start thinking about whether or not you'll make the putt. You play only one shot at a time, and you want to play it 100%. Just concentrate on hitting the wedge up close to the pin. You'll have several minutes in between to concentrate on the putt. But thinking about the putt while hitting the wedge shot will only hurt the latter.

Above all, remember to play with desire, determination and confidence. Sure, you'll hit bad shots. Golf is a relative game. The less you have progressed, the more shots you'll hit poorly. A newcomer will hit so many bad shots that it will be quite frustrating to him. But he should take this in stride and remain determined and confident. It's just a matter of time before he will be hitting 90% of his shots well instead of 10%. Learning to play golf properly is a matter of time, patience and endurance. The more you play, the better you will get. It's a long hard path. I would certainly hate to have to start all over again. Luckily for me, I began golfing while still a small boy. But many have taken up the game late in life and within a few years have become excellent players.

The main thing is not to become discouraged. It's a wonderful game and a "pleasant walk in the country" whether you score well or not. And you'll always score better if you take that "tiger" attitude I am talking about. Don't be a kitten on the course—be a tiger.

Doug Ford holds the Professional Golfers Association's championship trophy after defeating Cary Middlecoff in the 1955 finals.

Chapter Twelve

Chatting About Golf

Every once in a while, someone will ask me:

"Doug, what has been your biggest thrill in professional golf?"

Of course, most men who have played the tour for as long as I have—14 years—can look back on many highlights and probably just as many low points. Golf is a game of ups and downs—hot days and cold days—and you simply have to take them in your stride.

Naturally, it's most pleasant to look back on the best days. Two of my biggest victories were in the 1955 PGA match play event and the 1957 Masters tournament at the famous and beautiful Augusta National course.

THE PGA CHAMPIONSHIP

The 1955 PGA tournament was played at a fine course—Meadowbrook Country Club in Northville, Michigan. I figured my game was ready because I had played well the two previous weeks, tying for sixth with Dow Finsterwald in the St. Paul Open and then finishing 12th in the Miller Open in Milwaukee. My eight rounds in those two tournaments had all been between 67 and 71 and I felt I might be ready for a hot week. It came in the PGA at Northville.

In my first two matches I beat George Fazio and Ted Kroll, both by scores of 2 and 1. Then I caught Wally Ulrich on an off day and trimmed him 12 and 10. That put me in the quarterfinals and I never dreamed that my last three victories would be so decisive. I got past Fred Hawkins 5 and 4, then beat Shelly Mayfield 4 and 3 in the semifinals. In the finals my opponent was that year's Masters champion, Cary Middlecoff, who had triumphed the previous week in Milwaukee and was really playing fine golf. Cary had eliminated Tommy Bolt 4 and 3 in his semifinal match. However, in the championship match, I managed to outscore Cary and chalk up another 4 and 3 victory.

When I defended my PGA title in July of 1956, at the Blue Hill Golf Club, in Canton, Mass., I managed only two victories before being eliminated in the third round 5 and 3 by one of the greatest match players of all time, Walter Burkemo. But Jackie Burke Jr. was the eventual winner of the tournament.

The PGA match play events, which later were replaced by an annual medal play tournament, will be fondly remembered by all of the pros who enjoyed playing in them. Man against man competition is intriguing and a real challenge. When you're out there in a medal play event— which seems to be most popular with the galleries—you have little idea what place you're in. There's no sense playing against somebody who is somewhere else on the course.

You simply must play your own game against par and let the victories fall where they may. If you shoot 274 for 72 holes, for example, that's pretty good golf. And if somebody else shoots 273, he wins and there's nothing you can do about it. It's simply each man against the course and you have to play your own game. That is, unless you happen to be battling for the lead on the final day with somebody in your own threesome.

In match play competition, however, you're playing head-on-head with your rival. You're matching tee shots with him, trying to hit your irons closer to the pin than he does. And you're trying to knock in your putt to put extra pressure on him when he steps up to his.

Some fine golfers actually use very interesting strategy in match play. For example, I have seen golfers use a spoon off the tee just so they could be short of their opponent's

Doug Ford helps Arnold Palmer don the coveted green jacket, symbol of a Masters champion. Ford joined the exclusive "green jacket" club in 1957. Palmer beat Ford by a stroke in the 1958 Masters tournament.

drive. That gives them first crack at the approach shot, and if they can stick their iron shot up there close it puts that much more pressure on the longer driver who has to hit second.

Match play golf is a lot of fun and that's why amateurs enjoy using it in their weekend matches and for many of their tournaments. The Professional Golfers Association has been considering establishing a new match play event in Florida in a winter month. I think it would be a welcome and interesting addition to the tournament circuit.

VICTORY IN THE MASTERS

My biggest stroke play victory, as I mentioned earlier, came in the 1957 Masters at Augusta, Georgia. In 1956, I had tied for sixth in the Masters, when Jackie Burke won it, and I was hoping I could break through in '57 and win the coveted green jacket—the symbol of a Masters champion, worn only by members of one of golf's most exclusive groups. It is the ambition of every golfer to wear that jacket, I am sure.

Again, I was confident because I had been playing fairly well. I had just finished tying for ninth in the Azalea Open, won by Arnold Palmer.

In the first round of the Masters, I shot a 72 and, since scores were running slightly high, I was only a stroke behind Burke, the leader. I missed a couple of key putts in the second round and took a 73. That put me at 145 and I was five strokes behind Slammin' Sam Snead, who took the lead by firing a blazing 68 on the long (6,980 yards) and challenging Masters course.

Another 72 in the third round put me at 217 and only three strokes behind Snead, who had suffered through a 74 during one of those bad days on the greens. I was only three shots back, within striking distance of my coveted Masters title, but I was just one of the boys. What a log-jam had been created Snead was at 214, Harvey Ward Jr., Arnold Palmer and Stan Leonard at 215, Ed Furgol at 216 and Jimmy Demaret, Jack Burke and me at 217.

What a pack going into the final round! Certainly any of us could win. This was really going to be a wide open battle.

When I came off the 18th green, I could hardly believe what had happened. I had shot one of the best competitive rounds of my life, a six-under-par 66, to win by three strokes. It was one of those days when everything went right. On the 18th hole I finished with a birdie by holing out from a sand trap, as I mentioned earlier in the book.

Meanwhile Snead was closing with a 72 for second place, Demaret with a 70 for third place and Ward with a 73 for fourth. Some of the players I had really expected trouble from had just the opposite kind of round from mine. Furgol and Burke came in with 74s, Palmer with a 76 and Leonard with a 78. But those fellows came back in other years and proved their ability to conquer the great Masters course.

That 66 in the closing round of 1957 was the kind of a Masters finish you always dream about but never really expect. I needed only 25 putts on the 18 holes—14 on the front nine and 11 on the back.

But my wedge was actually my best club that day. On the ninth hole I blasted from a trap to within inches of the pin to cinch a par. Then I sank a 25-foot wedge shot from back of the water on the 12th hole after clouting a 6-iron over the green. Then came that sand trap shot on the 18th, which I sank from about 30 feet away.

Sportswriters asked me why I went for the hole from the bunker bordering the 18th. After all, I had a three stroke lead. A bogey would have been good enough. But, really I was just trying to get up close enough for one putt. If you do that often enough, the odds are that once in a while you're going to sink some of those explosion shots.

I'm considered one of the faster players in golf. I got a kick out of one writer describing me as "the guy who always looks as though he's playing through the group he's playing with."

I developed the habit of playing fast when I was a youngster in New York. At that time, Gene Sarazen's saying "miss 'em quick" was very popular. As a kid in New York, I caddied or worked in a golf shop. When I got through in the evening, I had to play fast to get in my round before dark. Some nights I'd go out with only about 90 minutes of light remaining and play 18 holes.

I also feel that the less I fuss around before swinging, the more I limit the tension that can destroy a good shot.

Tension, as you know, can seriously hurt your golf game and your score. Freedom from tension comes with confidence—knowing that you can hit the shot well and then stepping up there and hitting it with a positive attitude.

I sincerely hope this book will give you the knowledge and confidence you need to hit good wedge shots. They're stroke savers and I would like nothing better than to see you go out on the course and save a few strokes. Good luck.